Beyond the Fire

Also by Mary Leader

Red Signature
The Penultimate Suitor

Beyond the Fire

Mary Leader

Shearsman Books
Exeter

Published in the United Kingdom in 2010 by
Shearsman Books Ltd
58 Velwell Road
Exeter EX4 4LD

ISBN 978-1-84861-122-1
First Edition

Gratitude is due to the editors of the following publications, in which versions of some of this material, at times under different titles, first appeared:

American Literary Review: 'Shaker's Bereavement'; *American Poetry Review*: 'Husbandry'; 'Linen Repeatedly Folded'; 'Three Tortoises'; 'Ubi Sunt' *Antioch Review*: 'Education for the Likes of Civilization'; *Beloit Poetry Journal*: 'They Vibrate'; 'Letter to Arkady Plotnitsky'; 'To Gaze Is to Think'; *Cimarron Review*: 'Folio'; *Connecticut Review*: 'Fable'; *The Iowa Review*: 'Lulling'; 'Patronymic'; 'Winter Grasses'; *The Journal*: 'Among Things Held at Arm's Length'; *Pindelyboz*: 'Poem'; 'Mnemosyne'; 'Rosh Hashanah Sutra'; *Pleiades*: 'Envoi'; Pool: 'Emblem'; 'On Boston Common'; *Puerto del Sol*: 'Archeologist's Wife's Diary of which Two Entries Survive'; *River City*: 'Acquisition'; *Sagetrieb*: 'Linnet'; *Shearsman*: 'Death of a Gypsy'; 'Ending with a Spell Incised on a Rib of Scrimshaw'; 'Harvest'; 'Reel to Coax a Woodcarver's Ghost'; *Sonora Review*: 'Bride, Wife, Widow'; *Virginia Quarterly Review*: 'Balm'; 'Mimesis'; *Yale Review*: 'Bit from Possible Origin of Punch & Judy'; 'Dire Prophecy in Her Childhood Sealed'; 'Tallit with Stripes from the Book of Judges'

The author expresses her sincere thanks to the Center for Creative Endeavors in the College of Liberal Arts at Purdue University. She also acknowledges her deep debt to individual people who made the most direct difference in whether and how this book was written: Joel Bettridge, S. Beth Bishop, Mary Molinary, Daniel Morris, Joshua Phillips, Donald Platt, Dana Roeser, Lee Sharkey, Mark Yakich, and most of all,
Neal Leader.

Contents

I.

II.

III.

for

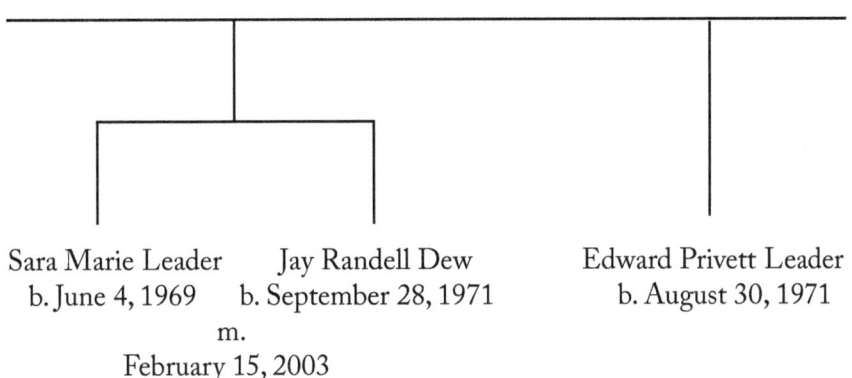

Sara Marie Leader
b. June 4, 1969

Jay Randell Dew
b. September 28, 1971

m.
February 15, 2003

Edward Privett Leader
b. August 30, 1971

And then bargain wth ye wind
To discharge what is behind.

—George Herbert, "L'Envoy"

I.

Tallit with Stripes from the Book of Judges

There was this place famous for its dye, the most
Prized of which was blue. The fabrics often came out
Fuchsia or marine or morocco or bruise or lavender.
The fences and furrows were a brownish blue.
Storms and berries were the exact colors of each other.
And every warrior among the returning wears
A prey of divers colours of needlework
A certain occupied barn was especially purple
Because a little girl there knew all about adult love affairs.
The grown woman there knew a cold, vengeful rage.
One time the girl hanged herself from a violet rafter
When she had had about all she could take. The woman
Climbed up and lifted the body from the noose.
She sprinkled it liberally with a clear liquid. Then
A little repentance entered the woman's heart,
But too late: the girl had already come back to life.
In a perfect fury they fought, tooth, nail, and shuttle,
And with the most marvelous results. Once the mad
Shredding was over and done with, two piles of threads,
Verily heaps of skeins, beautiful, lay.
The pair set to work. Girls and women elsewhere
Likewise set up their looms, stretched the warp
Good and tight, and their cloth was in no way inferior.
But nothing lasts forever, especially preparation.
Sad come the days of greatest relief and happiness
When men's mothers strain at festooned windows,
Of divers colours of needlework on both sides,
Meet for the necks of them that take the spoil.
The fences and furrows were a bluish brown.
Storms and berries were the exact opposite of white.
The fabrics came out fuchsia, morocco, or marine,
Bruise, lavender, or maroon. But the most prized was blue.
There was a city, famous for its dye.

Poem

Brittle. Wind is old news. But it is my

news nonetheless today when I say it.

They come, they blow, minutes; they are dry, dry,

they skedaddle across the white-dashed line.

Leaf scraps, leaf spinal cords. I'm a woman

not like, but with, the season concluding.

Leaves, leaves brittle-blown aslant the highway

not for the first time nor yet for the last.

Turtles and porcupines are part of it,

then entrails tattered. The crows' part of it

Enacts itself moving before car-roar

which I, machination, energy, and

Materials cause. Crows lift but return

right after. Thus they make their livelihood.

Bride, Wife, Widow

I adore the way
He hums when he shaves, his
Deep voice, his small, lotioned hands.

I detest the way he hums when he shaves,
His deep voice, his small
Lotioned hands.

I miss the way he hummed
When he shaved, or did any
Small thing with his hands.

Education for the Likes of Civilization

I have one I stitched when I was a little girl,
One I stitched when I was a teenager,
And one that somebody else stitched, which
Hung on the wall in my Granny's dining room.

"Stitched" is the term, not "sewed," for samplers.
I mention it because it is the same
Word the Greeks had for poetry, somehow.
Hemi-stichs. Something like that. I forget.

Wait a second. Is it "stitched" or is it "worked"?
I was supposed to know that, but I forgot.
De minimus non curat lex.
The law does not take account of trifles.

Small things are not dealt with by law.
If I make things small enough, I can escape.
If I make things as big as I like, I am in
Trouble. Blue is prettier but red is better.

They Vibrate

redblueredblueredblueredblueredblueredblueredblueredblueredblueredblue
narrowbroadnarrowbroadnarrowbroadnarrowbroadnarrowbroadnarrowbroa
WarloveWarloveWarloveWarloveWarloveWarloveWarlovewarLovewarlo
AresAphroditeAresAphroditeAresAphroditeAresAphroditeAresAphroditeA
marsvenusmarsvenusMarsvenusMArsvesuviusMARSvenusmarssunevmars
MortalVenialMortalVenialMortalVenialMortalVenialMortalVenialMortalV
arteryveinarteryveinarteryveinarteryveinarteryveinarteryveinarte
redblueredblueredblauredblaurotblaurotblaurotblaurotblaurotblauredbluere
roseirisroseirisroseirisroseirisroseIrisroseIrisRoseirisroseIrisroseirisErosIre
whorevirginwhorevirginredblueredvirginwhovirginblueorereadblueredblur
blueredblueredblueredblueredblueredblueredblueredblueredblueredbluered
foregroundbackgroundforegroundbackgroundredgroundbluegroundredblue
WaagrechtBlauHorizontalBlueWaagrechtBlauHorizonBlueNarrowRedLine
narrowbroadnarrowbroadnarrowbroadmarrowbroadnarrowboardnarrowwide
whybecausewhybecausewhyBecauseWhybecausewhybecausewhybegotuse
AQAQAQAQAQAQAQAQAQAQAQAQAQAQAQAQAQ
cresttroughcresttroughcrestroughcresttroughcrestroughcresTtroughcresTrue
shehesheheshelterSheheshehesheheshehesheheshehesheheshehesheheshehes
hesheheshehesheheshehesheheshehesheheshehesheheshehesheheshehe
comingovercominGovercomiNGovercomINGovercomingovercomingoverO
harimharimharimharimharimharimharimharimharimharimharimharim
ThouIThouIThouIThouIThouIThouIThouIThouIThouithouIthouItthouitTho
ergoifergoifergoifergoifergoifergoifergoifergoifergoifergoifergoifergo
straightcurvestraightcurvestraightcurvestraightcurvedstraightencurvestraight
particlewaveparticlewaveparticlewaveparticlewaveparticlewayparticlewave
boatwaterboatwaterboatwayboatafterboatwhatboatwavebowwaterboatwater
redblueredblueredblueredblueredbluerredderbluestreddestbluesredbluereed

Linen Repeatedly Folded

I am an old woman bare to the waist with red-orange flowers in her hair
It may be possible to deconstruct them
Fruitfully I am
A little girl but my present tense is a globe

I am a little girl bare to the waist with red-orange flowers in her hair
What luck to be talking early
I am an old woman as you know but
I am almost finished with the parallels

Right now in my bed is a shy ruddy girl
I see two graybeards of about the same height walking at the same pace
Together coming to see me but
I seem to have concluded that I am almost done with the parallels

Swans and a stag in the stream near the English village called Privett
So strange to me I barely say a word
Nor walk the herb-edged path to reach the Magen-David design
Nor touch the stele on which it is carved

Nor be offered the wine you buy to warm another woman's bloodstream
And although my present tense is not nebulous or noncommittal
I feel no glimmer of what it will be like when next I have clarity
The sun bounces blinding off a butter-knife blade

I am bare to the waist without red-orange flowers simple enough
Soon now the first cold days will come coughing
Like the man on Liebigstrasse with acne scars and tuberculosis
I had not yet understood that in the context of opposites I want to be

Well let me back up
I only know I mean to go farther
Will you also drop the negative valence with which trim is charged
I want to show you what happens when trim is operative

In the landscapes again the patches are present on the ground
Which is tilted up toward the eye rendering perspective suppressed
I agree with you that *Paysage de Champrovent* is particularly fine
Here is where I am feeling the pinch of e-mail

You are nodding or shaking your head quizzical or bored patient or not
I have seen you both of each of these
A figure is like a doll a chesspiece a candlestick in Balthus or the cat
Therefore there is much more room

The ages have this as their provinces surely the
Way a mother holds a baby incorporated into a breathlessly long series
So I am after eschewing the cult of the individual
I am sorry in different hands

As you said the old woman and the little girl being brought into proximity
Near but not identical
Intersecting triangles identical pieces in opposite positions interlocking
I am still confused about it and still involved with the parallels

But my present tense is becoming a globe
I can only hope that the amber pendant I ordered will arrive in time
The sun with its saber is poised
Rose Steinberg is my opposite name

Letter to Arkady Plotnitsky

Chicago, July, 2008
Germanium has indirect gaps.
Sun-points punctuate these geraniums.

Germanium can be doped with copper.
Geraniums can be red; these are.

Something about bulk germanium
As opposed to very very thin
Layers of it buried in silicon, measuring

Intensity against shift, then repeating
The measurements, Raman intensity, Raman

Shift, for various thicknesses of germanium
(Grown at different temps). Germanium and
Geraniums, then. Both said

To be grown. Paintings being flat should look
Flat. In lifeism, these geraniums

Are red and the fence behind them is blue-gray.
This coffee's wonderfully wonderfully bitter, 'tis.
Ramen noodles are good and cheap. It costs

Nothing to read these warm geraniums.
It costs zero to look at a library book:

The Principles of Physical Optics. If a painting
Looks like nothing so much as a painting,
That is the ultimate realism. That is why

I would paint these geraniums blue-gray
And the fence behind them red. Click on, click on.

Click on. Germanium may be ultrapure or
Germanium may be an impurity. Does Ga
Stand for Germanium? Does GaAs

Stand for Gap Absorption(s)? Kandinsky's
Painting *Waagrecht Blau* (1929).

Almost the whole painting is blue, but the small
Square is red and hence foregrounded. That
Is its/his prerogative. *Waagrecht Blau*

(Horizontal Blue). *Physical Optics*
WITH TEN PLATES AND 280 DIAGRAMS

Important as a cat's yawn, lovely and true.
Munich, July, 1913
"Surrounded, perhaps for the last time, by

The summer beauties of nature I send you and yours
A farewell greeting. Your old friend, Ernst Mach"

To Gaze Is to Think

Wait long enough, and a pattern emerges: the same
Series of light and dark bands that Young saw.

Nothing but moving patterns of intensities: bright
Here, brighter there, dim elsewhere;

Imposed; the sunny mist, the luminous gloom
Of Pluto; even as when I fix my attention

On a white house or a gray bare hill or rather
On a long ridge that runs out of sight each way,

How often I want the German unübersetzbar
(Untranslatable). The rays long-pale slanting—

Late, conveying loss, nostalgia, an end to
Things (untranslatable). I well know it.

And the face overspread with light, with swimming
Phantom light overspread but rimmed and circled

By a silver thread. The pretended sight-sensation
(Translatable) whether visible or invisible (untranslatable);

How often I want its intensity: and the slant
Night-shower driving loud and fast. The invisible light

Which abides in the brain-marrow or, visible,
In sundry rotten mackerel and other smashy matters

And the sun great whirling explosive, and van
Gogh's starry night squeezed into fine tendrils

Of optical fiber, and then perceptual light
From monitor screen, this fair luminous mist,

This beautiful and beauty-making power, light,
And light's effluence, cloud at once and shower;

The use of thin washes applied with a brush
Or thick slabs of paint laid on with a spatula

Or multiple planes of transparent and opaque rock
Color: the velvety whites, the shining blacks,

The ambivalent grays, the ghostly undulations;
Light's valleys and hills. A smile, as foreign to,

As detached from the gloom of countenance, as any
I have seen. A small spot of light travels

Slowly and sadly along the top, when all
Below has been dark with the storm. Stupor.

Brow-hanging, shoe-contemplative, strange.
No matter what great distance we measure for any

Voyage of light, to itself it covers no distance
At all. The 30,000 feet from Everest's peak

To sea-level, the 3,000 trillion miles from
The red star Betelgeuse to Earth, the twelve inches

That light covers in a nanosecond; all,
All are one and the same to a traveler on laudanum

Or a photon, who sees the universe approach. At the speed
Of light, at that critical speed, all lengths

Contract to zero, and the traveler sees an infinitely
Thin cosmos. I drink fears like wormwood,

Smell cement of rain and cloth. And what is
Succession with inter-space in the undivided

Indivisible duration? The traveler and
The traveled differ only in their wave-lengths.

Wave, lengths, the distance between consecutive crests.
What is a moment? This I will say: Some

Were brilliant beyond belief, as when the last
Log before dawn would spark into my mania.

Linnet

To approach, upon poetry as a subject, the venerable Allen R. Grossman

I am prepared to resist the need for an aesthetic of declamation.
  I am prepared to embrace the need for an aesthetic of declamation.
I am prepared to avoid slighting any of my current ambitions.
  I am prepared to surrender any and all of my deepest ambitions.

  I shall wear the plainest clothes I own: a long ochre skirt,
Boots broken in, a shirt and tie. I will not pretend to knowledge
  Beyond my ken, but neither will I apologize for the things I think of.
Stein, Dickinson, I ask you to be with me; my own name, be with me: a

Risen sun.

Queen of Heaven

Rose, Climbing, Lily, Tiger. Ladies named Garnet & Opal. Me named for
Several Mary's, including the main one, Our Lady, including my mother's
Mother, an exact spell: Mary Bryce Privett.
Grandfather would   try to soothe me:
"You got some really   hard words up there."
Those perennial flowers, name of "Bachelors' Buttons," the petals of whose
Blossoms were fringy, nice and soft to the touch, came in solid colors, also
In versions that were   ever so slightly striped,
Like the colors of   sucked peppermints,
Or like the tiny lines   of capillaries spidered
On the noses and cheeks of old Irish people. A color family. The blooms,
Like many ceramic madonnas, came in sweetest blue, in lilac, cream, pink,
And featured in were   some more vivid, i.e.
A deep magenta,   or a royal blue,
And those I invariably   made sure to include
Against the pastel predominance in the bouquets I would pick at Granny's
Request (and to her hand-clasped delight!) then put in water in a jelly glass.
Mary: the rose-tree.
Mary: the dawn.
Mary: the gate.
Mary: the root.
Mary: the grape.
Mary: the wheat.
Mary: the fount.
Mary: the temple.
Mary: the shrine.
Mary: the beacon.
Mary: the mirror.

Mnemosyne

It must have been when I was around eight **T**hat my heart started to hurt in my stomach. I do **K**now I loved the house *before* the redecoration. **T**he kitchen linoleum was a spatter design **I**n primary colors plus black. Bright **S**pecks & splotches & dots, I associated with **T**he feeling of a circus. The experience of a circus **W**as something else. But black was the touch I liked **B**est, very black spatters as accents on a ground **O**f fire-engine-red/china-dish-blue/marigold-yellow. **C**opper platters, hung as pictures, showed **S**cenes out of the interiors of Dutch taverns or **H**omes; they shone in the firelight; they had **F**ireplaces in them; they shone in the light from our **F**ire, our own fireplace and everything matched: **T**he curtains & the divan showed Pennsylvania Dutch **F**arm scenes in red, green, ochre, and again, **A** great black, printed on unbleached muslin. **L**ater I feel scared sick when I think of **T**he putrid green countertops that followed, **I**ntervening. Years saw the time for which Easter **S**napshots had to be taken despite misery on the **P**aternal face, stoniness on the maternal, and on **T**he little brother's both tanned cheeks, tears **U**pon tears, a solid gleam. Then there was the time in snow, **O**r what had been snow and then was slush, **H**er having grabbed the nearest coat and made **A** run for it, for what? just "it." She fell. It was just so sad. **G**ot mud on her shins, on the beige poplin coat, **T**hough not on the raccoon collar. I should know; it was my coat. It was my senior year, last of my eighteen living with her. **S**he was mad at me, even recently. **W**hen Dad had his stroke and she was surrounded by **H**is relatives, her enemies; she was mad at *me*. **I** am the one who says so. Looking back, I suspect **M**y mind was attractive. Just in time I know this. **B**lack-blacks like Manet's, and the Spaniards' before him, **A**nd Motherwell's after him. Ideas like Mondriaan. **E**xcept that I didn't leave out spatters from lines **A**ll the time; sometimes, yes. I dubbed **M**y watercolor series CIRCUS but was pretty **S**ure it was not original with me. Maybe **D**erived from Rainbo® bread. The fluid tints **W**ould merrily flick off the oval top of the brush; **T**hat's all I know. The gesture of the wrist was **C**ertainly borrowed, familiar from watching **T**he hands of the priest when Holy Water **W**as required in addition to the bangle-sounding **A**roma of Incense. In fourth grade, I plagiarized

From the book *Famous Paintings for Children* **B**ut I forgive myself. It was just **T**hat I loved the Rembrandt so, the woman **F**ramed in the top half of a Dutch door. **I** at least had the sense to leave out the word *__C__hiaroscuro* since it was obviously beyond me. **I** think the woman-in-the-top-half-of-a-Dutch-door **W**as looking slightly off to the side, out of **T**he sides of her eyes, definitely gently smiling. **S**he was backlit in saffron. She was capped. **W**as she capped? Either she was capped, or her hair **W**as pinned back, or both. I knew her well.

Death of a Gypsy

A woman of the winds anticipates
Bartering old harmonies for sheep, sheep
For wool, wool for cloth, cloth for paraphrase,
Common language for a spell of godspeed;

Trade trade trade until she coins! Redundance
Is not possible but repetition
Is. She gets caught outside in the thunder,
Departs, like lightning, with a last vision:

The morning star, soaked with feeling derived
From rivers of cobalt-glazed pottery,
Points to the caravan she has outlived
As it loops back! She is not forgotten!

Her skilled mother, next to her young uncle:
"Là!" Pink and gray. There! The first cathedral.

Autobiography

Lookee. My mother, by clipping and saving Erma
Bombeck's column from the *Tulsa World*, Sept. 21,
1969 (I was a mother myself by then) inadvertently
Kept, on the verso, a kind of prediction of what,
As it turned out, I called my first book of poems*.

DENVER, Colo. (AP) — Friends of Mrs. Louise Shanley, who recently retired as a clerk in the Colorado Revenue Department, always know when they get a note from her even though it has no conventional signature.

Mrs. Shanley's signature is a woman's face drawn in blue ink with red hair. Mrs. Shanley's hair is red.

**Red Signature* (Graywolf 1997).

P.S. My hair was red.

As a Signature is to the work of art,
So the work of art is to Art.
As the Work of art is to art,
So a life is to Life.

Shaker's Bereavement

The loop went up around the sky and you
Were In it, you, I'm sure, the color blue,
A dark blue, the stilldark blue—the sun!
Had not arrived. Blue, the chosen one,
Who knew since it was In you, past the cold.
And They knew, the Prophets knew, foretold.
I all but saw the slew. And I believe
I felt the loop—it trembled, gripped my sleeve,
It gasped but—lost all doubt which route to take—
The speed, the angle, when, and For Whose Sake.

Color
the
chosen
past.
Knew,
be
my
route
for
And.

The bereavement

went up around the sky and you were In
It, you, I'm sure, the color blue, a dark
Blue, a still, dark blue. The sun had not
Arrived. Blue, the chosen one, who knew
Since it was In you, past the cold and They
Knew, the Prophets new-foretold. I all
But felt the slew, and I believe. I saw
The loop it trembled gripped my sleeve it gasped
But lost the doubt the route the route the speed,
The angle when and for whose sake the loop.

[Year 33]
In the
darkening,
knowing
naught, we
felt gasped
speed. Whose?

Mimesis

What were those? Those were fiery
Craters.
No, those were the nights of childhood.

Madness and sky clung together
In that sleep
And surrender.
Surely you've been there many times before.
You've come a long way just to hang back.

Those were rosary beads glowing out of the dark.
No, those were the nights of childhood.
No, those were fiery craters.

Balm

The hip bone's connected to the (beat) thigh bone.
The thigh bone's connected to the (beat) knee bone.
The knee bone's connected to the (beat) shin bone.
Now hear the words of the Lord.

I said to Laura,
"I don't see how novels can get written, they're so long."
"You just form a relationship with it," she said,
Tossing her really really shiny straight hair,
"Like you do with your body, you know?
You do the things that are good for it,
Don't do the things that are bad for it, you know,
Like you can't *not* have a good relationship with

Your own body."
"Oh."
First I slapped my face and chest
Until they were red and stinging.

Then I yanked from its hook in the bathroom
The pretty nightgown, the thin nightgown
With all those little tucks, the nightgown
Sprayed with Obsession perfume for a man
Who never showed. And I ripped it in two,
In four, in a dozen pieces, two dozen pieces—
How the pearl buttons flew!
Then I stabbed my hand with my pen—

This was during the loud groaning—
But the pen merely broke, so I took
And smeared the ink all over my tongue and
My cheeks, mixed in with the general tears.

What a sight!
That's whom I saw in the mirror then,
When I struck a match and lit the eyelet trim
On the yoke of her real nightgown,
The ugly flannel nightgown she had on,
'That filthy girl on fire can't move!' and so
An invisible woman comes to her rescue,
Dashes, with cupped palms, water upon her.

And so they got to the dawn, rocking.
And got to a psychiatrist within the week.
Now I wash every day, to remember.
I remember every day

With the clean white towel,
With the almond-scented lotion:
The toe bone's connected to the (there)
Foot bone; the foot bone's connected to
The (there) ankle bone;
The ankle bone's connected to the (there) shin bone.
Now hear the
The comforting sound of crickets.

II.

Rosh Hashanah Sutra

"Therefore on this day you shall do no work of service,
And it shall be to you a day of impressive sound."
—Numbers 29:1

Gold-bell Shofar;
Wind-stir Shofar;
Plane-nearing Shofar;
Car-passing Shofar;
Crows-in-next-tree Shofar;
Plane-farring Shofar;
Cough Shofar;
Fart Shofar;
Violin Shofar;
Urgent-unnamed-bird Shofar;
Manhole-cover-struck-by-tire-quickly-lifted-set-down Shofar;
Man-and-woman-passionately-but-not-violently-arguing Shofars;
Footfalls-upstairs Shofar;
She-who-pronounces-the-words-honey-cake Shofar;
Kettle Shofar;
Doorbell Shofar;
Stack-of-plates Shofar;
So-called silence Shofar;
Deep-voiced Shofar;
A-man-on-the-porch Shofar;
Ladle Shofar (metal, tapped on pot edge);
Ladle Shofar (wooden, dry, set in clean tureen);
Ladle Shofar (wooden wet-from-washing-damp-from-drying set on table);
Crows-in-neighbors'-trees Shofar;
Shofar of We-chant-loud-in-tight-circle-in-interior-stairwell;
Shofar of We-chant-softly-in-loose-circle-in-opened-conservatory;
Wind-settle Shofar;
Tea-or-brook Shofar;
Hammer Shofar (blows in sets of two and three);

Jaylike Shofar;
Sparrowlike Shofar;
Computer-printer-pounding Shofar;
Squawker Shofar;
Wind-swell Shofar;
Apple-biting, or "Hunger," Shofar;
Ritual apple-biting Shofar;
Ambulance Shofar;
Two-whoop-squad-car Shofar;
Rhododendron-rustles-before-leaves-fall Shofar;
Dogwood-rustles-in-fall/human-remembers-4-part-white-blossoms
Shofar;
Indrawn-breath Shofar;
Shofar Effortless;
Shofar Effortful;
Giggling Shofar;
Crying Shofar;
Barking Shofar (intermitted);
Inaudible-moan Shofar;
Nearly-inaudible-grunt-from-teacher Shofar;
Central-heat-coming-on Shofar (gentle numbered clicks);
Black-bell Shofar.

Cello Concerto

Commencing with percussion

wet-wood oars clunked down on dry-wood plank:
he will let the cello/boat drift, will drift with it,
mid-river, heartsick, too full of hope over an old
friend's niece, spending her year, front left upstairs
room in a house near campus, girl lovely at tennis,
saying over creamy coffee "your serve is amazing";
meanwhile his wife, furious, thumping batter
in a wooden bowl, late, later, feigned sleep now their
midnight harmonics are all in the past . . . passage
for cello and bamboo flute transposed to noon, to
dissonance for cello and silver flute, for rusted harp
and knives: metallic fall; when the moon dawns
in the sun's place begin the river-risen-on-the-cypresses
theme, for cello, bassoon, receding flood, and then
the winter coming down: cadenza for early ache
and someone else's violin; icicle daggers from his
one-story roof: icicle marimba along a certain
upstairs window melting into . . . a shared tour of
fountains, but silence in his dreams in scenes that
should be noisy: women ovalling unvoiced wails,
rocking fruitless baskets; him mouthing *ahh!* stabbing
bloodless sheep . . . summer wearing on: oboe insistent
on c# minor, rattle punctuating cello line . . . another
autumn: brass-cymbal-roll-leaf-blow; last slow
melody: cello, thunder-sloping timpani, paired
sopranos, rain: he steals from one house into
the other, he spills how much he wants the girl
a woman, how much he wants the woman stayed.

Cuneiform

for Shama Aziz

Young man's fortune

You will let joy and music swell
Filling every gap
Two or three days later
You will leave
You will now sit down
Scarcely knowing what you have done

The young man describes his intended to his father as though she were some kind of bird

She withholds the date of the death of a semilegendary poet
She is distance
She will destroy above
She begs off with the urulla reed of the maltster
Her chest is rust yearly
She is bright of eye
She is a matrix of specific eggs
She makes the puny grow
Her understanding is such that if I could intuit it and reject it
It would damn nothing

"When I miss him the most" [fragment]

When then proceeding north

From _[place name]_ for 25 _[units of distance?]_
upon a mountain path

When [illegible] overflows everywhere

When
[There is a considerable break in the tablet]

When I pluck fleece of the right and of the left

When I find a small number of colored pebbles

When I have been calculating

When I sit on a golden throne / when I eat at a table of
lapis lazuli

When I hunt the ox in the brush

When in the alley outside the hour being late I hear
a wandering musician

The young man describes his intended to his bosom-friend as though she were night weather

She is a cloud pouring on one of the ridges
The rain is over and the moon is shining
She lets the heart be light on the left
She lets the apex of the heart be light on the left
In darkness she advances
The darkness has not yet touched my heart
It is a terrible thought
Nights of chilly rain when colors are not seen
The threads put in her hands by the fates
Are intricate to handle
Her footsteps are in harmony with the summer stars
She brings the surf to my bedside
The threads along which blindly her fingers move
Seem extremely intricate to handle

Young woman's potion

If the station is long
If the princely days are long
You will be long
You will be uncompromising fidelity
I will be fog
You will appeal to me

Husbandry

for Jennifer & Max Toperzer
m. August 8, 1998

"Honey? I think maybe we should move this coleus… Honey?"

"What."

"I said I think we might want to move this coleus."

"Okay."

"Because I know it said partial sun or partial shade or whatever but I just don't think it likes it behind that rock."

"I said 'okay.'"

Ubi Sunt

Chance led me that morning to a secluded gallery.
Certainly I was glad to be dead. It explained a lot.
And it allowed me to harangue every daub. You there.
You're too intense. Hey you, you're too prolonged.

You. Yeah, you. You're too alone. What's your rush?
Probably they did not deserve all this crit. No color ever
Manufactured would do for meaninglessness. Well.
I have my own table. My own table and nothing

To say or eat. Pretty river. Lists. In the end it was all of it.
A little girl weeping without a plan, gone on the train
With her grandparents, her mother impossibly near
On the other side of the glass oblong. Resemblance

Clear. . . . .lost now to me month after
Month after tree upon tree upon bridge after tree
After month upon bridge after day then several bridges
Close together, as over the Arne enmapped, too small to

Take, as in Take the Queensborough Bridge. At any rate
I'd rather look at something tired. This bonnet is old.
This lady was skating. Did this boy rise to a Cardinalate?
Dunno. This fly has a cherry; this fly had a cherry; this

Today a white truck replaces a yellow car. Tomorrow a void,
Utterly unpainful, will replace my face. Yesterday a white
Dress replaced a yellow skull. Even God, a realist if not
Exactly a representationalist, had or has only shadows for holes.

Grandfather-aged fathers are nothing new. Gerhard Richter.
Abraham. Norman Mailer, Larry Brown, or visit any cemetery:
To be sure there's a man named Josiah or somesuch
Alongside his three wives in a row. Child of his old age

But not usually hers. . . . . lost to me now. Lost
To me then. Speech, speech. Their child is named
After the town where she, the bride, rather recently,
Went to college, or "attended," as he would say.

Even dead, I try to defend myself with a smirk.
Was this time a city or a countryside? Let's see:
Were there planes or geese? What were we nearing?
What three parts has a leaf? Because of a snapshot,

Because of a set of parents, I know a dress of dotted swiss.
White dots upon fabric of navy blue. Little boats, yes?
More like waves, no? More like umlauts. No. I am not that
Locatable and Rembrandt probably never heard of

Dotted swiss if indeed such even existed then and who
Cares anyway what tense we're in and my brown velvet gown
May cover me over sans marker and it shall not obtain
To anyone else to drink my sweet wine, Greensleeves.

Ending with a Spell Incised on a Rib of Scrimshaw

The thing is, I thought the proclamation bruited
        That you were to be the ruler and the dance was to be
Anything, even sleep. You had kempt shoes. And.
        Were alone again. As was I. Come midnight, I
Dipped the sponge, dropped water drops upon
        My collarbone, asked imagination: *Over at your house,*

Does my image ever whistle through, just another sailor?
        Or. Are you or are you not the token tree,
The head of some triumphal avenue? Even now,
        Thoughts of you cause me to know lyric's
True compound, close-afar, give rise in me to
        Memories of a time preceding you. Of. The last

Farewell in bed put the wonderful doings into my history,
        Said last being none other than a drover, rough,
Who had me in Wales. I would have been your most
        Precise friend, if not your enchantment, the winding of
Your air. I'd have tolerated affairs, real or make-believe,
        Or some of each, and in the long run, in quotidian old

Age, I'd have looked at you as an attorney looks at his watch.
        But. You married another. This midday, I am forced
To ring forth in language shaven from the bindery,
        Merely to pretend I could write: "Beloved. Leap from
My hold to my gaze—O free, O feline-like—instead of
        From gaze to hold, and that will be just as good."

On Boston Common

for Arlene J. Johnson

On Boston Common, the saints are doing their walking meditation
while the angels try to sell them
Red Sox pennants and doves. What a racket they make, those angels,
let alone the doves.
When the saints stay on course, though, then the angels quit bugging
them and congregate on steps and benches,
Delighting in holding seashells over their ears and the ears of their
friends. For saints,
It helps their confidence to hold in a left or right palm a smooth
stone, lifted from a bed
In the formal garden, chosen after naps. Angels tend to fidget, their
voice-mail unheeded
Left and right, thinking Damn! Saints are beings who are through, yet
still going. Angels are through beings, period.
Through air, through aether, they can coast, they can dive straight up,
they can fall.
Serene the solitude of saints may or may not be. But certainly angels
feel solitude through and through
As perfectionism heading directly for rage. One archangel has been
given Hunger
For her name. Her anger is pure anger, unalloyable with silence. She has
to be drugged with Commonal, thudded
Into sleep, her omnipresent ecstasy banished, to irrupt in dreams of
tunneling flight.
In point of fact, hunger is held in joint tenancy by angels and saints. The
difference is only that saints
Sit around an empty table, eyes at half-mast, aware of which of
their members can best take the pain
At any given moment, whereas angels act like the next-to-last hyena
snatching the last morsel of gazelle,
Off through human-waist-high grass to a patch of bald ground invisible
from twenty feet away.
Many saints remember glory; some were great spinners in their day. But
now, their hearts lift off, but not the rest

Of their bodies. Helicopters make them cry. Even though they know
from mercy, saints
Can't *require* anything, can't *demonstrate* how peace is helped by mercy.
Helicopters make them cry.
Nothing human is alien to them. Angels question whether peace by
definition means staying
Apart. Oh sure, they see the saints always hanging together, together
and apart. But not one angel
In a hundred comprehends how the combination can be. In times of
human war,
You'll hear angels railing at statues of saints, screaming, "*Do* something!
Do something!" But saints are so ultra-human,
They cannot lose any one by preferring any other. On the Common,
toward evening,
Over by the pond, the angels finally confront the saints. One angel
demands to know, "How can we, of all people,
Be expected to understand peace when we are so aggravated, so full of
want?" Saint Tearbringer,
A former tailor in whose presence sorrow comes forth, opines, "You
already have the answer, inside you."
"Oh, go fuck yourself, Tearbringer," is *an* answer from somebody.
Another angel protests,
"Hey, rapture has its tears as well as anguish has its tears, you know."
"Yes," says the saint. "Nothing
Angelic is alien to me." Well, on hearing that, the archangel Hunger just
loses it:
"*Everything* angelic is alien to you." Tearbringer and Hunger stand
searching into each other's eyes.
Simply, there's nothing else to be said. Later, soon, once Hunger and
the other
Angels in attendance this summer, along with all their swan cousins,
lie down to sleep, distributed there
On the water's bank, then Tearbringer, and the other resident saints, come
and steal in among them,
To lie down too, interspersing, so that through the night, their somber
robes and the glossy white wings
Make a chessboard, of gray and gray, camouflage, to tax the eye, to baffle
the hand, of God.

Fable

Who is it there, stirring about, chiming upon
The Book of Lamentations? A tall man, Rabbi Leib,
Disguised as a peasant, goes into the kitchen,
Takes up the lantern, goes into the yard.
The pitch of the ax-blows seems higher
For the wood being frozen hard and for
The silence encompassing them
And all along you can hear his voice:
Lord, remember what has happened to us.
Flakes of bark, frozen brittle,
Stick to the Rabbi's knitted gloves.
He continues reciting:
Princes have been hanged at their hands;
The face of the old has not been respected.
With his load, his years, and the winter,
He makes but slow progress.
Youths have toiled at the mill;
Boys have collapsed under loads of wood.
Who else stirs about? This one,
Poor man of poor men,
Young widower, young father, his child
Fevered, his candle low, his fireplace ashen.
The double rap at his door,
Though late, is like someone from next-door,
Like his brother-in-law
Coming for Shabbat back when.
On his shoulder, the baby girl
Rolls her face, frustrated-like. He
Cracks the door, nudging the threshold of snow
An inch or two, saying, "What is it?"
He hears the burden in the voice
That answers, "It's just that I've been trying
All day to sell this lousy load of wood.
At this point, I could let you have it
At a real bargain price."

We drink our own water—at a price;
We have to pay for what is our own firewood.
The family man, though desperate, says
"Sorry, I'm a little short of the ready
Right now." He took a step to shut the door,
Didn't want the peddler inside, and all this time
The baby fussing and wiggling in his arms
And slow—slower than ever before—snow fell.
"So, I'm in no hurry," spoke the visitor,
"I can come back another time for the money.
At this point, you'd be doing me a favor."
"Well . . ." Given this much encouragement,
The rabbi stooped in under the—did I mention
Rabbi Leib was unusually tall, and also broad—
Stooped in under the lintel.
No mezuzah on the jamb but who cares?
He lowered the bundle of wood to the hearth
And went about building a small fire,
Humming as he worked, and the child,
Who loved humming, relaxed toward sleep,
And her papa gentled her down in her cot.
The sound in her chest was like a broom.
What happens at midnight?
A young father is jerked out of sleep—
The sound of the broom has stopped.
What else happens at midnight?
An exhausted tall man, sucks air through
His teeth—he can't seem to stop shivering—
Lips moving, repeating from the source-text:
You cannot mean to forget us forever.
You cannot mean to abandon us for good.

Three People who Broke their Hearts from Bewilderment

"Mon panache."
—Final line, *Cyrano de Bergerac*, by Edmond Rostand

Featured Speaker at Poetry Festival in Norman, Oklahoma

Tall black man listening to his famous late father's voice on tape
Often closes his lips and nods yes, and afterwards, after
The applause for the tape has died down, weaves
Remarks and quotations, some of which are as follows:

The man* was just magnificent

My father wrote long** poems

The son and nephew of

Preachers and Scholars

An axe of lightning

Great God A'mighty

Like a bear on fire

Some say he was born in Georgia

Some say in Alabam'

*Melvin B. Tolson

**lahhhng: slide up on vowel; down on "n"; play
on making "long" long

Open mic reader who acknowledges Schizophrenia as her disease

Pale girl in black velvet hat with large white plume atop
Spiky bleached hair does indeed read with trembling hands and
With intercoiled facial confusion and without tears and without
Suppression of tears, her poem whose closure goes:

She called me
a dumb-ass
but I forgive her
because she's
a stupid human
who knows very little
if anything

Open mic reader who explains that her maiden name was Innis

Old white lady, whose unmarried name (she may or may not know
This) means Island in Irish, when introducing her poem by relating
An encounter between herself returning home after many years and
"A little ol' black man on the road," uses the latter's speech, points
As evidently he had done in the event: "That *there*'s the Innis Place"
And adding "We called him Cap'n" and "Yessir I mean yes ma'am,
We'd see that *green*, and we'd say 'Them's George Innis's alfalfa
Fields,'" and she, quoting that, has her voice suspended by emotion
But, she doesn't break down and cry until she arrives at the very last
Of the phrases that are actually *in* her poem:

Wild plums
On the ground there
For our savoring.

Three Tortoises

I'm
 sick of
This chewing,
 this having to
Chew: never too much
 or too little; always
The verge: too little too much.

So
As to
 shut up, that's
Why I lug this
 heaviness. Other-
Wise, I might start shrieking;
 all men would cover both ears.

I'm tired, log-tired, and I wish
 it would dew. Since I am
Unsightly and must
 stay hidden, I'd
Like at least
 to feel
Clean.

Dire Prophecy in her Childhood Sealed

she will go to live in a warehouse where
blouses are being made with illegal dyes
in day-glo colors, so bright they are stiff,
while they, the unhappily laughing young
Women who work there, after initially

assessing her as a threat, soon accept her
as she is: poor, old, unlikely to report
blouses soaked in the vats, abandoned
in the fluid until it dyes even the buttons:
Violet, orange, hot pink, lizard green;

she will have her own room, though,
not so bad. But three kerosene lamps
occupy the nightstand. A television set
is on, live wire! and in her clumsiness,
She keeps knocking things over, my God,

how negligent someone is, kerosene
right down the hall from blouses still
dripping chemicals, polyester smell like
ocular migraine. And it's not as if there's
An outside, a just-beginning-to-snow.

Trinities

In the child's still life, the triangle
Thrusts straight up, points straight up.
The plum's stem, enlarged, forms a post
To wick Our Lord's pain from the ground.
Two radishes and a red paraffin seal stylize
Into wounds. A bird nest traps
By promising protection.
Claws, talons, feet coexist on the ceiling.
Michael, Anthony, Francis look three ways.

Grapes, pears, leaves watch from above.
The trinity comprises justice, compulsion, place;
Dripping is no fourth. Time ceases or else
Time dissolves.
What is imminent? The blue violet
Lance or knitting needle is about to puncture
The perfect black disc,
Disc from which will tumble, scatter,
Disc from which will spray

A thousand deadly stinging tips.
Those in the same
Plane with the disc
Survive. They are in the computer.
I am the first one
To feel being struck.
No one before me
Has felt
Me being struck.

Bit from Possible Origin of Punch & Judy

Adam meets Eve
And before he even
Hears her side of the story,
He gives her up

To the prosecution.
Then he turns his back
On her, tossing behind him
A too-small fig leaf,

Muttering "Cover yourself."
She puts the leaf
In front of her face.
That always gets a big laugh.

Harvest

*A found ballad**

Three months before the war started
        Mildred Aldrich, who was sixty-
One, had said that she wanted quiet,
        Calm and perfect peace.

She found a peasant's house with open
        Rafters and a hazel hedge
In Huiry, a hamlet thirty miles
        Outside Paris. Her small garden

Looked out over the valley of the Marne:
        Over grain and sugar-beet fields,
Orchards and asparagus beds. From her house
        She saw the Battle of the Marne

In September. She saw the French and English
        Fighting the Germans, and the Germans'
Defeat. She saw the artillery fires,
        Palls of smoke, bombs,

Fires, and dead soldiers. She wrote
        A book about it called *A Hilltop*
On the Marne, which was published in 1915
        And went into seventeen printings.

*Souhami, Diana. *Gertrude and Alice*, London: Pandora Press (1991), p. 122

Archeologist's Wife's Diary of which Two Entries Survive

<<< >>>

It was not without emotion
That we entered the City of Puna,
The tumult & bustle of the capital
Of the Marata Empire, towards evening.
Sir Walter Scott, with all his powers
Of description, would be at a loss here.

<<< >>>

On looking into the cave—
Immense. Ponderous—dark—
You can hardly make anything out.
A kind of giant wooden umbrella—
Wet clothes hanging up to dry.
Stone carved away—
Not architecture—but sculpture.
Baffling. & we both
Quietly sneaked out of Paradise.

<<< >>>

Emblem

for Lynette C. Black

The apple between the moon of stripping and the moon of seeming pleased
The etching showing a violet's yellow eye connected to the sun
The rainfall like a barcarole rippling down the man's back
The news that devours me whole both body and grief
The beauty of rot whether deciduous or evergreen
The understanding I gain within a figured bass
The plucking from the garden as I sing it
The thirteen principles of Maimonides
The peach-pit on the soft palate
The earliest (known) sonata
The Snow on the Gorse

Border for a Small Child's Cloak in a Time of War

Pumpkin, we
Don't fear that
Thundering,
Just think
Of angels' carts, white
Carts that
Pass in fog,
In
Fog that,
Like the wheatfield, shudders
Where wind
Divides it. See?
Bootsy
Likes our
Cozy hearth. Hear him
Purr? And
Listen, inside the
Wood,
The red
Embers cough, as our
Soldiers do
When they come
Walking
Through here,
Through here past your
Grandpa, and
The other Elders,
All
Lined up
On great big horses!

Persistence of Empire in the Dream of the Pastoral

Today in Woodwode I'm searching out the nine closest-
Together trees—these here, I think—and around
Their trunks one by one I move, a spool—

Red grosgrain—in my right hand, and in my wake—
Blue—a nice loose shank of rope narrow of
Gauge. I take precautions. I walk in reverse
As I let these things out, one riband trailing
My unindented waist, the other perched

At the pinnacle of my dominant arm's reach.
I—counter—clock—wise—pass.
So far, so good. There. Back

Where I started, only to remember I have
No knot-craft! None! Still, I try unprettily
To connect my cordy beginnings with
My cordy ends. Later it gets in my mind
That I'm supposed to—compelled to—insure I focus

Exclusively on this work. But even spiders
Lose concentration once in a while surely.
So next day I take up shears, the ones with the green

Plastic handles, and return to Woodwode where
I snip, where I pull down in loops, in cascades, in
Festoons, the artifice. It's all I can do not
To re-skein the lot, carry the rich fibers home
With me. I resist solely in recognition that

I might be tempted to name my threads after two of
The wind twins, or name one Fire and one Water,
Or think in terms of the beloved mapped highways/

Rivers. Or, say, England and America or
Roger King and Miriam Chief or even just
Red and Blue. It's no easy matter, this,
Collapsing cross-legged, sitting, shredding slippery
Silk into a mound of vermilion fluff,

Untwisting nylon climbing strands into filaments
Wire-like, curvy-stiff, cutting those into pieces
Yea-long, measured with calipers of thumb/forefinger.

Now keepable? Not really. I mean,
For what? I worry, though, that left in place,
Even this stuff disassembled from my olden ritual
Could cause, well, rather more harm than good.
All in all I decide to cast the remainders

Toward new shrubs. Let them be caught or not,
On thistles, on squirrel-winter-tails, on thorns.
Let them be rained upon until, in runnels,

Their dyes run off, or be dried up, covered up, by dirt,
Or again be windborne, now called Farther and Further.
This way, my leavings may end up providing
Downiness—gules, couchant—for bird-nest activity,
And/or pikes—azure, rampant—for ants' crusades.

III.

Reel to Coax a Woodcarver's Ghost

   sight experiments for butterflies
Inlaid blackberry
         (sight must thorn phantasm)
   cedar butterflies in wilderness
Butterflies pervaded sunset

         (proof in the mortal thorn)
   sunset and wainscot
Cedar numbs phantasm
         (inlaid cedar butterflies benumbs)
   dark of berry in cedarwood

Proof on the floor
         (shavings pervaded)
   pale of cedar in butterflywood
Mortal phantasm in sight
         (we have underpitied)

Folio

Consider the distinctions among aether and air and oxygen within a hundred breaths of death

*

I mean, normally, the outer sphere of heavenly edge whether imaginary in myth or actual in imagery from the Hubble Telescope (see, "aether"), and the grand earthly surrounding supply (see, "air"), are lovely—taken for granted—containing and expanding as they do—but when it comes down to it, the true necessity to keep life from stopping is the O (see, "oxygen")

*

Molecule, element, fundament

*

And, well, she has that

*

Oxygen not straight from a tube at this late stage but *oxygen* as usual enwebbed in *air*, two terms out of the three I posited to start this poem

*

But, then, she does keep returning her stare to point to the corner above her and to her left, at an angle of about 11:00 o'clock from her face, the left-hand corner away from the door, away from me, where I in the tableau stand by her right side and I have to say, this anonymous room seems an odd place for her—who noted corners all her life—to regard one more corner in

*

For all I know, it is—*not* oxygen—but the waiting for a corner's three planes coming together to dissolve and reform into a section of the aether-sphere—*that* O—which is the most necessary of the necessities within a hundred breaths of death

*

Or, simply, the word "corner" occupies her mind as it blinks

*

Her body is at issue: flesh, bone, ignored hair

*

Her jaw, slack, a slide-rule, shifts to the left, shifts to the right, shifts like the jaw of a goat, a goat tied to a post, off to the side at a horse show

*

Her teeth, loose pebbles, studs in brackish water, saliva pooled dark as tobacco

*

Teeth wet, shit wet

*

Liquid shit a symptom to do with a shut pancreas causing this spreading stink inside her, outside her, beyond any time when she managed any form of ingestion

*

Could be there's something *wrong* with that corner

*

I am *guessing* "within a hundred breaths of death"

*

The point is, on that question of "since when," of "within X number of breaths," neither she, the dyer, nor I, the counter, can have retrospect from here

*

My Irish forebears, who came to this country in ships, listed on the ship's manifest, or had listed for them from dictation, their names, the names of their wives (if any), the number of their children, their status whether convict or not and (if so) of what crime, and finally, their reason for leaving—"High Rents & Oppression"—writing one after another "High Rents & Oppression," copying it in, some of them resorting to ditto marks following those who wrote High Rents and Oppression before them—and all who made the voyage and lived to tell of it must have moved from *There it is!* to *We are there,* to *We got there. . .*— to *We got here*—in that generation, if not longer, "We," not "I"

*

That was time, they say, that is the way of time and I apply that to death now

*

Who are those people, the uninvolved, the not included, seeing in with sheer glances from the edge-blackened envelope of the hall, emigrants or immigrants

*

But they have rights, nurse's aides, heavy or thin, housekeeping, other people's relations

*

That is how ignorant I am, thinking those folk are somehow avatars of pertinence, whereas she knows, it is not from the hall that the fetch will come but from that corner

*

When did her skull grow forehead-knobs

*

When did her brunette eyelashes become barely existent

*

You could visit every stone effigy and every brass to be rubbed in England, lords and ladies, queens and kings, knights and the dogs at their feet, and never would you see an eyelash represented

*

If only it could have been her *own* corner, in her own bedroom

*

We are not even at the Pawnee Hospital, site of many a stay among us, where her father had long reigned as Doc Haddox, but at the one in Cushing, locus of her arch-nemesis self-righteous sister-in-law, my aunt Armand, who had said to me, taking the phone away from Mother—my mother who was saying, "I've never felt pain like this" but I did not, did not come then! did not call the airline *immediately* but instead hung around Emory all weekend entertaining myself and hoping to run into the boy, yes boy, not even a graduate student, on whom I had a ridiculous crush and preparing for teaching classes for which I was shamefully underpaid—I owed Emory no loyalty; I received none from them—I owed that boy no love; I received none from him—yet I gave both unworthies precedence! at what cost, what cost to know for the rest of my life that I did not fly to my mother's bedside, did not *hear* her telling me "Come, daughter, for I am dying" *mea culpa! I mean it, mea maxima culpa* and Aunt Armand in the Cushing hospital, commandeering the phone to *tattle*, saying to me "Mary Bryce, she won't eat a thing" in intonations of "She's still the same spoiled brat she always was"

*

If only Mother had uttered "Mother," her mother, loyalty personified, or "Daddy," the two of them always the greatest of favorites to each other, or her "second mother," Aunt Sara *Aunt Sara*
? (see, "imagined waiting-in-suspense"), that is how naïve I am

*

No story, no "rattle," no wisp, not a sigh

*

I had to quit humming and bend down and look at her chest in silhouette to see if it was moving: it was hard to tell; it was so subtle; it was imaginable that the chest was still ever so slightly rising and falling; I finally had to conclude: I had missed it, her actual last breath

*

Within 24 hours, I will insist that a poem of Mother's be put on the card the funeral home will print and I will personally take over the choice

*

Within eleven years, I will forgive Armand, whose own skull, in her nineties, under skin so fair it belongs only to those born with red hair, supplies her cheekbone-knobs, which mine match

*

And of self-forgiveness, that part of the Janus figure stays inchoate

Winter Grasses

These we have studied
These by their colors
Copper Silver Bronze
Gold Nickel Platinum Brass
While metals and those
Who worshipped metals warred
Upon the plains the drenched
Grasses stayed low
While whose once glittering
Turrets and domes
Turned green copper and felt
Their sharp details blunt
The grasses befriended
Rain wind dust snow wind
And were rewarded a way
To change without corrosion
To this day they move
In wind as our hair moves
As it would have moved
Their horsehair plumes
Their feathered breastplates
Their slenderbladed halos
As these things rouse us
As windgrass rouses coyotes
As roused their dogs
As wind lifts
As wind parts the fur
As jackrabbit hunches
As kestrel shoulder tufts
As crow wingtip riffles
As we listen with all of
Our ears winter grasses

Acquisition

A tourist stops for gas. His hat is slick on the inside rim from hair tonic;
his wife parts her hair in the middle and wears
A hairpiece called a rat around which she wraps her own sable brown

Hair to form a bun. They've stopped for film, stopped for magazines,
stopped for Murder Mysteries or Juicy
Fruit Gum or Five El Versos. They've stopped for lunch. Their child

Would like the grilled cheese sandwich, please. They are Catholic, part
of a tiny cluster in Pawnee where Catholics are called
Catlickers. The wife was what Granny said, a cradle Catholic, but

The husband converted to it. His family, when they went, went to
the Methodist. That was next-biggest
After the Baptist. The only one small as the Catholic was the Nazarene

And that was for poor people. Child wears to Mass gloves of white
cotton with bumpy white embroidery and at
The pulse of each wrist a buttonhole keeps getting stretched out when

Fooled with or fiddled with and then it won't stay put on its mother-
of-pearl button. Like Momma-Granny-&-Aunt-Sara,
This small one wears to Mass a petite hat, trimmed with artificial

Flowers, usually pink, or blue or white or yellow. Were the flowers
pretty? Is it possible to say? Friday's child,
Loving and giving, looks at hats and at the couple from every angle

Available to her and from any distance she can get. She has long since
learnt to read. She is not as easy to fool as they
Think. They are together. The father's father was a good provider, and

That is what he's trying to be. He does not owe-money-all-over-town.
Plus whenever they stop for the night, it is always
At a Best Western, if they have one, and in Gallup, New Mexico, they did,

And then they would look for a nice restrunt. The mother looks away
from the way her husband chews. Her husband
Gnaws his food; he gnaws his cigars. His wife shaves her legs, plucks

Her eyebrows, reads her mysteries and also her paperback whose cover
said Naked in the Sun. "Naked," like "Baked."
To pass still more time in the front passenger seat she shapes her nails

With a silver-sharp thing. She tolerates her husband's hair tonic,
green in its bottle, H-A Hair Arranger.
The smoke from his El Versos is overpowering, but even so, she feels she

Should say she likes "the smell of a cigar" and does say that to various
people. His nose is pug. Her nose is pointy.
She is quick and he is slow. She can hardly refrain from ramming a fork

Down his throat. He wishes he could shove her right into the lake. When
little Mary Bryce Privett
Draws them, she doesn't put them on the same piece of paper but makes

Pairs of pictures. On one of the couple's wedding anniversaries, she
inscribes the picture of the bride
She has made for Momma "Happy Anaversery from Someone who Loves

You." She inscribes the picture of the groom she has made for Daddy
"Happy Anaversery from
Someone who Loves You." She doesn't say whom in either case. Both

Drawings survive, each figure shown in profile, as is typical of a certain
stage of development in children's
Drawings of people and animals. Also extant are four decks of cards,

Depicting Seasons, with the two Jokers marked "Hi" and "Lo" in case
of playing pitch which is, unlike bridge,
A "Hilarious Game"; and six apparently indispensable frayed towels in

Maroon to match the edging tiles; and a shaky El Verso box full of nubs
of crayons, multitudinous nubs of crayons,
Except that that's not what they were, really. They were My Crayolas.

Among Things Held at Arm's Length

FATHER	MOTHER
m. February 14, 1947	
Joe Hauser Privett	Katharine Jo Haddox Privett
July 29, 1921~January 22, 1996	May 29, 1924~January 22, 1995
He was a good sport &	"My children were
His hair was red.	English-speaking islands."
When plaque broke loose	—from her diary
In arteries and caused	
Stroke, he would call	"like, years later, reading
Plaque "flak." That's how	lines I wrote so unfamiliar
He perceived it.	I think, amazed,
He had a purple heart.	How did I come on that?"
When he was a kid,	—from one of her poems
Thirteen- and fourteen-	
Hour days on the tractor	"I think even when light dies
Meant he got sunburned,	[stanza break]
Badly, even dangerously,	and the bones of the stars
Right through his shirt.	are piled up in cairns
When he put these two	in the sea
Things together, talking	[no stanza break]
To his daughter, which	a part of me
Time-frame was he in?	will not be old"
"They thought I was gonna die."	—from another of her poems
Said solemnly, like a child.	How did she come on that?

Pawnee, Oklahoma

Lulling

For two voices

"They're just not holding out any hope at all now."
They'd stopped even the i.v. By the time I got there,
My mother was so dehydrated, she couldn't
Cry. It had been snowing all day, not that the blinds
Had been opened. Too dehydrated to cry,
But when they moved her, she sobbed.

By 10 p.m., my brothers and their wives and kids,	She sobbed
Our last uncle and all our aunts had cleared out.	All now
Neal went to the lobby to read. Her room was dim,	To cry
Now, thankfully, after a forty-five minute ordeal	Got there
In the brightest possible glare, three nurses	The blinds
Taking increasingly anxious turns trying to restore	She couldn't

A slipped Heparin lock to my mother's elusive vein.	To restore
Finally! One of the nurses, relieved, telling her	And kids
"I'm gonna tape that down real good now,	Three nurses
So's you don't have to go through that again."	Cleared out
Too dehydrated to swallow, Mother nodded,	Minute ordeal
Nodded as she had to me earlier, when I said	Was dim

"I love you." Too dehydrated to say hardly anything,	I said
She groaned "I love—uhhn—you too—uhhn. Uhhhn."	Elusive vein
"She likes you to stroke her forehead," Neal had said.	Mother nodded
Neal gone out to the lobby, the rest gone home,	Telling her
The white sheets, the minutes into the morphine,	That again
And me in the den-like gloom, preparing to settle.	Good now

I went over to my bag for my book and my shawl.	To settle
But first I needed to get a good look at her, and so	Hardly anything
She opened her eyes. And just fractionally,	The morphine
Turned her face toward me. She watched	Uhhn. Uhhhn
My hand as it went to stroke her forehead. I knew	Gone home
Myself to be shadowy because she followed	Had said

The alien hand with her flattened eyes	She followed
As an infant at night follows a mobile's shadows	My shawl
In the light from the hall. Of the song she sang me	I knew
When I was small, I remembered mainly	And so
The tune: hmm hm-m swe-et Afton la da dah, da dum	She watched
Hm hm hmm.... Hm hm hmm, flo-w-gently....	Just fractionally

Her forehead so dry and stretched with pain,	Just fractionally she followed
I stroked, and hummed and hummed, past the time	She watched my shawl
When one of her long, long breaths did not return.	And so I knew

Patronymic

No sighted person

Hasn't been affected by the action of
Wind on some kind of banner, streamer, flag, wind-
Sock, piece of fishing line left after a wind-

Chime has gotten knocked down or taken down or
Been blown down off of its hook under the eaves,
Or on branches bare, and branches bearing leaves

Such as sycamore, plum, black locust, scrub oak,
And branches bearing needles and cones, such as
Red cedar, cedar of Lebanon, spruce. No

Hearing person hasn't been affected, some
Time or other, by the sound of wind, of _____,
Of _____ ___, of ____. Many have not remarked

Being affected thus.

You know, Dad, I still

Have the brown-and-white banded feather I found
Out at the old barn. The barn, vacated now.
I remember his description of the heat

Coming off the galvanized aluminum
Siding (or was it tin?) when he alongside
His brothers nailed it to the frame their father

Had designed and constructed. A "natural
Engineer." "Third-grade education, but he
Could do our algebra problems." "He couldn't

Tell you how he got the answer but he always
Got it right." That barn had, indeed has, "a
Self-supporting roof." Fire took the foursquare

House this grandfather of mine ("Pop" to his kids)
Likewise designed and built with the boys' help,
The girls bringing iced tea. Out in the country

Like that, once the town's one fire truck runs out of
Water. . . . At least it didn't spread to the barn,
Nor to the silo. I took the feather to

The hospital to show my father, one of
The last times I saw him on this earth. "Look, Dad,
I found this out at the Old Barn. Do you know

What kind it is?" See, because by then there was
So little under his command, I thought it
Would be good to ask him things I knew he knew.

Amount in 'Bushel.' 'Gallon.' 'Peck.' The steps in
Bringing in the wheat. Terms, names of the different
Implements. Harrow. Hain. "Owl." He was never

One to make a big deal over nature. He
Was glad he could provide the answer, though. I,
In the rapid speech pattern I learned from my

Mother and her mother, kept on, "What kind of
Owl, Dad? Like a 'Barred Owl'? Or a 'Barn Owl'?" "Just
'Owl'," he said.

'Just owl.' He said. I think. But, as

I've been working on this poem forever (key-
Board slippage left of f, or keyboard slippage
Right—wind, or wing—"father" coming out "gather"),

It could be that only here does he say "just owl"
And in the actual air said something like
"I don't know, Sugar." Yet sensitive to me,

As always, "Might be some kind-of-a owl." His
Highest praise to me came when I'd made something
With materials—"Why, you're just as handy

As a pocket on a shirt"—his harshest
Criticism—"Don't be thattaway"—was for
When I was unhappy. Adults used to say

"Spittin image of her Daddy, ain't she?" and
"Smart as a whip" or "sharp as a tack." And to
Him, *Hello, Joe, what do you know, did you just*

Get back from Kokomo? Some see no need to
Remark being affected by a wind-swept
Field of vetch, or by a lone persimmon tree,

Or by, down a ways, rainy ditches with their
Cattails, cattails with their red-winged blackbirds' calls—
Emanations from the well-tempered shoulders.

Pentecost

It began with a sssssssssssss.
We thought we would hear a whhhhhhh
        like the wind.
We'd heard wind, and we knew wind,
        for relief;
        for fear;
        for bride-arrival;
        for harbinger;
        and for a vocable shroud.
This began with a ssssss,
        like a hissing rock.
Not one of us had but heard
        the wind at night,
The perception for I am alive inside
        the uncountable lives.
This was different.
We'd heard the wounded birds
        coming down from the sun;
We'd heard the psalms
        centrifuging into eternity;
We'd heard thunder;
We'd heard incorporeal fingers
        screeching in gravel miles away;
This was different;
        this was not the same.
We were as if fainted,
        in the midst of immense motion;
We were as if up swept,
        in the onrushing impetus;
The walls rippled our peripheral vision;
We groped for each other's
        flowing clothes.
Then we were none of us bound anymore,
        the roof simply was not

and the ceiling made no distinction.
We had no idea how long any of it took.
We still do not know how long.
The most outspoken among us
now says only
that the most outspoken
among us then
was heard to say:
"It is begun."

Envoi

The bottle to the wine said
I am green and you are red

The ivy to the wall said
I'm alive and you're not dead

The cat to the storm said
Do your worst above the bed

The band to the hand said
I'll turn gold when you are wed

The lamp to the page said
Close your eyes until you're read

www.ingramcontent.com/pod-product-compliance
Lightning Source LLC
Chambersburg PA
CBHW030048100426
42734CB00037B/582
9781848611221